THE *SUCCESSFUL* MAN'S VISION BOARD

Welcome to the book that is going to help you become every part of the successful man you want to be! Whether this is your first time diving into the world of manifestation and the power of vision boards, or you're a seasoned vision-boarder and looking for inspiration, we've got you covered.

OUR GIFT TO YOU

Along with the clip art and exercises in this book, we want to support you in keeping your energetic vibrations high, with the art of powerful affirmations and gratitude which is so important to the vision of the successful man you want to be. Incorporating these practices into a daily routine, as well as crafting your perfect Vision Board, is like pressing the fast-forward button on your manifestations.

As a thank you for getting this book, we'd like to offer you:

100 Gratitude Prompts

Keep your gratitude habit as powerful as possible with this mini book of amazing prompts.

Affirm Like A Boss

Learn the secrets of Manifestation, and take your affirmations to the next level with this guide.

To get access to these, scan the QR code.

WHO ARE MANIFESTATION PULSE AND HOW TO USE THIS BOOK

Manifestation Pulse was founded in 2021 with the purpose of empowering as many people as possible to make their wildest dreams a reality. Our team of experienced and dedicated coaches has helped hundreds of clients across the last 3 years to take back control of their destiny and rewrite what they believe is possible for them... and the results have been outrageously successful!

This book is our chance to share some of the secret sauce with you and provide you with the thinking and materials for you to create your own.

Vision Boards are a key tool that we've used with clients over the years to support them in manifesting a range of aspirations - from entirely new lives, new careers, and jobs that have people jumping out of bed in the morning, abundance in money, new lifestyle, and other desires - through to finding, and re-finding love, meeting their specific person (SP) and soul partner, along with so much more!

This book is split into three parts to help you develop your own powerful Vision Board:

1. The 'What,' 'Why' and 'How': An overview of Vision Boards and 'What' they are, 'Why' they work, and 'How' they work.

2. Understanding Your Goals: Two reflective exercises to help you gain clarity on what it is you want to manifest and why. These short practices are a fundamental part of your Vision Board journey so that you're building the vision board that really reflects your true goals and desires.

3. A range of powerful clip art: Photos and graphics that provide a connection with your successful man vision, alongside poignant words of affirmation and quotes.

SECTION 1: THE 'WHAT' 'WHY' AND 'HOW'

What are Vision Boards?

A Vision Board, otherwise known as an 'Action Board' looks simple but its effects are much more powerful and profound.

It is exactly what it sounds like - a board, in whatever size that works for you, containing specific visual representations of your goals across the areas of your life that really matter to you and your vision of success.

How Vision Boards Work - the art of Manifestation

Manifestation is the idea that your beliefs create your reality. As Gandhi once said, "Your beliefs become your thoughts, your thoughts become your words, your words become your actions, your actions become your values, and your values become your destiny."

This profound statement encapsulates the essence of manifestation, emphasizing that your subconscious beliefs are where you truly manifest from. A daily practice that supports and encourages these beliefs, such as Vision Boards, truly is a game changer as this practice helps align your subconscious mind with your desires, reinforcing positive thoughts and ultimately supporting you to manifest the life you desire.

And you're not alone. Some of the world's most successful men - from business leaders through to celebrities, actors, musicians, politicians and more have all used vision boards as part of their journey to where they are now.

Drake

In 2007, when Drake was still unsigned and mapping out his future, he searched online for "world's craziest residential pools." He fell in love with one of the homes that came up and set it as the desktop image of his computer.

In 2012, Drake purchased that very same property.

Jim Carrey

Before his acting career breakthrough, Jim Carrey's vision board took the form of a mocked-up $10 million cheque he wrote to himself for "acting services rendered", dated ten years in the future. He carried this cheque always in his wallet as a daily reminder and motivation to keep pushing for success. Exactly ten years later his role in the movie Dumb and Dumber gave him a cheque for precisely $10 million.

Steve Harvey

Has famously gone on record about his Vision Board success.

"Everything I've ever gotten in life, I've written. My vision board is crazy. You wound't even believe it because I'm not even in the need business anymore. What's on my vision board now is astronomical and guess what I'm gonna get all of it."

Why Vision Boards Work- The Neuroscience

When you focus on your goals through visual representations, it activates the reticular activating system (RAS) in your brain. This filtering mechanism helps you stay focused on what truly matters, while filtering out distractions. By keeping visual reminders of your aspirations, not only are you getting super clear on what you want to manifest, but your subconscious mind also stays aligned with your goals.

Vision boards work because they work directly with the law of attraction which states that *like attracts like*. So what you give your focus and energy to is what you attract back to you tenfold! By setting your intentions and goals through our Vision Boards you're communicating to the universe with complete clarity what you want to call in.

SECTION 2: UNDERSTANDING YOUR GOALS AND DESIRES

All right, the first thing we want you to do here is take a deep breath in and a deep breath out, because this right here is where you get to be as big, bold, and wild as you want. It's where you get to conjure and call forward your biggest dreams, even the ones you haven't voiced out loud until now.

So before we get into the crafting, creating, cutting, and sticking part, there are two exercises in this section to help you to discover the goals and desires that really align with you. This will be the helpful foundation when it comes to piecing together your vision boards, because when it comes to manifestation, the more specific you can be, the better!

We are our most magnetic (attracting the things we want) when we are manifesting from a place of authenticity, as opposed to ego (the things we think we "should" want). So get really honest with yourself here, be open to your success goals changing and adapting as you move through these exercises, and reconnect with what your 'successful man vision' really is on a deeper level.

EXERCISE 1:

Consider the 5 different categories below, rate each of them on a scale of 1-10 and outline how happy you are in these areas of your life. Make a note of what you would like to change within them.

Category

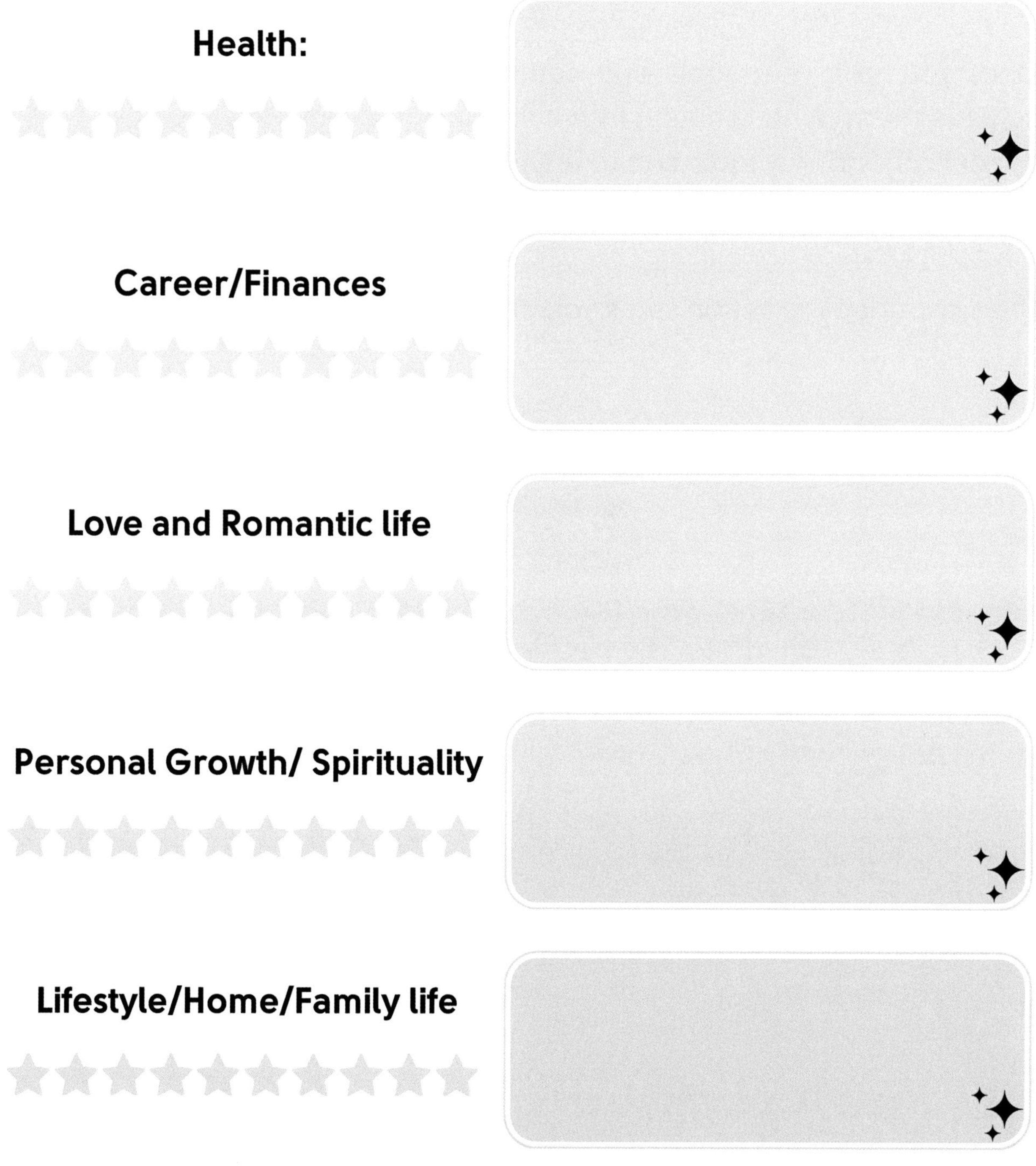

EXERCISE 2:

Now lets break this down even further

Using the spreadsheet on the next page, list all your goals. Don't worry if you don't have goals in all of the categories - it's the ones you really desire and have you so excited to receive that we want to map out here, as these will be going into your Vision Boards.

Once you have your goals, take some time to reflect on why you want to achieve them. What would it mean to you if you did? How would it benefit others? Pay attention to anything that could be coming from a place of ego or expectation and don't be afraid to challenge yourself if this comes up.

Then consider the action steps you can take to reach your goal.

Pro Tip:

Make sure the action steps are manageable to help you keep consistent with them. The best way to create habits is to gradually introduce them, instead of overwhelming yourself with lots all at once.

Category	Goal	Why	Actions	Target Date	Milestones
E.g. Health	Eating better	To feel more energetic each day. I want to feel focused in mind and body and not as sluggish.	• Research the food groups that I should be having more of / less of. • Exercise Regularly (minimum 3x times per week) • Sunday Meal Prep	Q3 This Year	✓Research healthy recipes ✓Join the gym ✓Start going once a week across the first 2 weeks, and then twice in next two weeks

Category	Goal	Why	Actions	Target Date	Milestones

Before we launch into the exciting part of the clip art, a few words of advice for Vision Boarding success:

1. Prepare Your Space: Find a quiet area and time where you can concentrate without interruptions. Your external environment is a reflection of your internal, so consider a space and time that will accommodate your full flow.

2. Reflect on Your Goals: Take some time for proper self-reflection and identify what you truly desire in different areas of your life. Feel free to come back to Exercise 1 and 2 whenever you feel called to reflect on your goals.

3. Gather Inspiration: This book has a lot of different options for your Vision Board but you may still want to collect specific magazines, photographs, quotes, or any other materials that resonate with your goals beyond the materials in this book. The more specific you can be the better. So for example if you are manifesting your SP (specific person), get really clear about what they look like (their eye color, their features),the unique and special things that you do together. Or if you're manifesting a new career, think about the type of chair you'll be sitting on and the view you're going to have.

4. Create Your Layout: Experiment with different arrangements before committing to one that feels visually appealing and inspiring.

5. Assemble Your Vision Board: Glue or pin down the chosen elements. Use a corkboard or poster board if you want your vision board to feel even more solid.

6. Find the spot that means you see it: Display your vision board in a place where you'll see it every day, such as your bedroom or living area. Make sure you are regularly engaging with it, visualizing the imagery coming to life.

7. Don't just create it, feel it! Lean into how it it will feel once your manifestation comes through. So, for example, if your goal is to become a CEO and an absolute powerhouse, connect with the essence of confidence and power of the version of you that has already achieved this. Give yourself permission to get excited about your life changing!

8. HAVE FUN! Creating Vision Boards should be about creatively expressing your desires and communicating them with the universe. It's an exciting and vibrant self development tool, so let loose, and have fun creating your board!

YOUR SUCCESSFUL MAN CLIP ART SELECTION

WORKOUT PLAN
Week 1
Week 2
Week 3
Monday
Tuesday
Wednesday

THIS WILL BE MY HEALTHIEST YEAR EVER!

HEALTHY st
LIFE rd

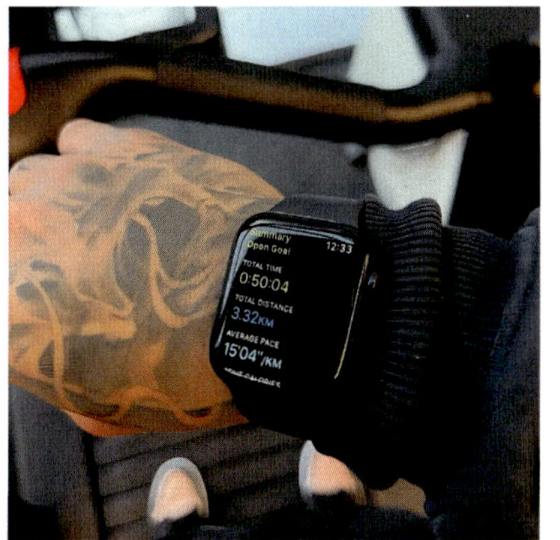
Open Goal
12:33
TOTAL TIME
0:50:04
TOTAL DISTANCE
3.32KM
AVERAGE PACE
15'04"/KM

I CAN
I WILL
I MUST

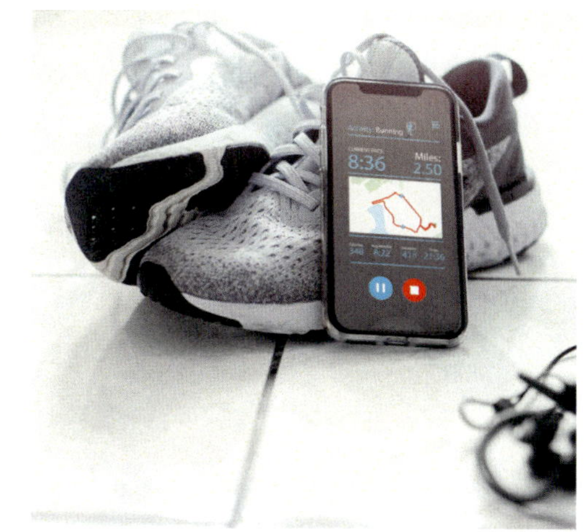

A BALANCED diet

HEALTHY is my vibe

Detox DAY

I AM COMMIMITED TO BECOMING THE STRONGEST & FITTEST VERSION OF MYSELF

I HAVE THE STRENGTH FOCUS AND DETERMINATION TO ACHIEVE MY FITNESS GOALS

EVERY DAY I AM SCULPTING MY BODY INTO THE MASTERPIECE I ENVISION

I FUEL MY BODY WITH THE RIGHT NUTRITION TO OPTIMIZE MY PERFORMANCE AND RECOVERY

I TAKE PRIDE IN PUSHING MY LIMITS AND EXCEEDING MY OWN EXPECTATIONS

I AM COMMITTED TO A LIFESTYLE OF HEALTH & STRENGTH VITALITY

DISCIPLINE AND CONSISTENCY IN MY FITNESS ROUTINE CREATE UNSTOPPABLE RESULTS

MY FITNESS JOURNEY IS A MARATHON NOT A SPRINT AND I AM IN IT FOR THE LONG HAUL

I REST WHEN NECESSARY KNOWING RECOVERY IS KEY TO MY GROWTH AND SUCCESS

MY BODY IS A REFLECTION OF MY DEDICATION AND HARD WORK

EVERY REP, SET AND MILE BUILDS A STRONGER HEALTHIER AND MORE POWERFUL ME

I EMBRACE CHALLENGES BECAUSE THEY MAKE ME STRONGER BOTH PHYSICALLY & MENTALLY

I AM TAKING CARE OF MYSELF

TAKE CARE
of your
BODY & SOUL

I AM **CONSTANTLY EVOLVING** AND BECOMING THE BEST VERSION OF **MYSELF EVERY DAY**

I AM **OPEN** TO **LEARNING** AND GROWING THROUGH EVERY **EXPERIENCE** IN MY **LIFE**

I EMBRACE **CHANGE** AS AN OPPORTUNITY FOR **GROWTH** AND **SELF-DISCOVERY**

I AM IN **TUNE** WITH MY **HIGHER** PURPOSE, AND I ALIGN MY **ACTIONS** WITH IT **DAILY**

I AM **CONNECTED** TO MY **INNER** WISDOM AND LISTEN TO THE **GUIDANCE** OF MY **INTUITION**

I AM **GROUNDED** PRESENT AND CONNECTED TO THE **PEACE WITHIN** ME

I ATTRACT **EXPERIENCES** AND PEOPLE THAT HELP ME **GROW** & **SPIRITUALLY** EMOTIONALLY

I **RELEASE** FEAR AND EMBRACE **LOVE** TRUSTING THAT THE **UNIVERSE** SUPPORTS MY **GROWTH**

I AM **CONSTANTLY EXPANDING** MY AWARENESS, AND I AM OPEN TO **NEW SPIRITUAL INSIGHTS**

I EMBRACE **MOMENTS** OF STILLNESS ALLOWING ME TO **CONNECT DEEPLY** WITH MY **INNER SELF**

I FORGIVE **MYSELF** AND **OTHERS** FREEING MYSELF FROM **PAST** BURDENS AND **GROWING** IN **PEACE**

I TRUST THE **UNIVERSE** TO GUIDE ME TOWARD MY **HIGHEST POTENTIAL**

amazing memories

Sweet
LOVE

partner
in
CRIME
We are
getting
married

WORLD'S
Best
DAD

CERTIFIED
COOL
DAD
SINCE MY BIRTH

My Kids
HAVE
PAWS

Choose your friends with *caution*

Plan your future with *purpose*

Frame your life with *faith*

I ATTRACT HEALTHY FULFILLING RELATIONSHIPS THAT BRINGS JOY AND GROWTH INTO MY LIFE

I ATTRACT PEOPLE WHO UPLIFT INSPIRE AND ENCOURAGE ME TO BE MY BEST SELF

I COMMUNICATE OPENLY AND HONESTLY BUILDING TRUST AND CONNECTION WITH OTHERS

I AM CONFIDENT IN EXPRESSING MY FEELINGS AND NEEDS IN MY RELATIONSHIPS

I AM PATIENT AND COMPASSIONATE ALLOWING MY RELATIONSHIPS TO THRIVE

I CREATE STRONG MEANINGFUL RELATIONSHIPS WITH THE PEOPLE IN MY LIFE

I AM DESERVING OF LOVE RESPECT AND DEEP EMOTIONAL CONNECTION

I NURTURE MY RELATIONSHIPS BY BEING PRESENT & ATTENTIVE LOVING

I AM OPEN TO GIVING AND RECEIVING LOVE IN A BALANCED AND HEALTHY WAY

I ATTRACT RELATIONSHIPS THAT ARE BASED ON MUTUAL TRUST RESPECT AND UNDERSTANDING

I AM FULLY COMMITTED TO GROWING AND EVOLVING ALONGSIDE MY PARTNER

I ATTRACT A PARTNER WHO VALUES AND SUPPORTS MY GROWTH AS MUCH AS I DO THEIRS

5

WE CANNOT BECOME WHAT WE WANT BY REMAINING WHAT WE ARE

I LIVE A **BALANCED** AND **FULFILLING** LIFESTYLE THAT **NURTURES** MY **MIND** BODY & **SOUL**

I CREATE A LIFE OF **ABUNDANCE** JOY AND PURPOSE THROUGH MY **DAILY CHOICES**

I CREATE A **LIFESTYLE** THAT BALANCES WORK PLAY AND **PERSONAL** GROWTH

I AM **INTENTIONAL** WITH MY **TIME** FOCUSING ON WHAT **TRULY** MATTERS **TO** ME

I **MAINTAIN** HEALTHY **HABITS** THAT SUPPORT MY **LONG-TERM** & **SUCCESS** HAPPINESS

I ATTRACT **POSITIVE** EXPERIENCES AND **PEOPLE** THAT **ENHANCE** MY **LIFESTYLE**

I LIVE IN **ALIGNMENT** WITH MY VALUES ATTRACTING **PEACE** & **SUCCESS** HAPPINESS

I **SURROUND** MYSELF WITH **POSITIVE** INFLUENCES THAT UPLIFT AND **INSPIRE** ME

I AM **OPEN** TO **NEW** EXPERIENCES THAT ENRICH MY **LIFE** AND **BROADEN** MY **PERSPECTIVE**

I **MANAGE** MY **TIME** AND **ENERGY** WISELY ALLOWING ME TO ENJOY A **FULFILLING** **LIFESTYLE**

I **INVEST** IN **MYSELF** KNOWING THAT PERSONAL **DEVELOPMENT** **ENHANCES** MY **LIFESTYLE**

I **FOCUS** ON **CREATING** LASTING MEMORIES NOT JUST **ACCUMULATING** MATERIAL **THINGS**

ONE WAY
NEW CAREER
NEW JOB
BRIGHT FUTURE

Capital
Analysis
Brainstorm
START-UP
Planning
Teamwork
Idea

WORK
FROM
HOME

FOLLOWERS

A GOAL IS A PERSONAL PROMISE TO YOUR FUTURE SELF

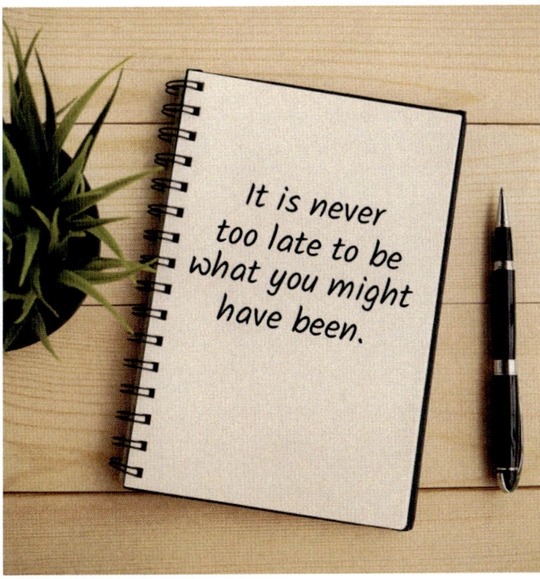
It is never too late to be what you might have been.

I AM CONFIDENT IN MY SKILLS AND ABILITIES TO SUCCEED IN MY CAREER

MY CAREER IS A JOURNEY AND I AM FULLY COMMITTED TO EXCELLING EVERY STEP OF THE WAY

I BUILD STRONG SUPPORTIVE RELATIONSHIPS WITH COLLEAGUES & MENTORS

EVERY DAY I AM MOVING CLOSER TO MY ULTIMATE CAREER SUCCESS

I AM OPEN TO LEARNING FROM EVERY EXPERIENCE MAKING ME A STRONGER PROFESSIONAL

I ATTRACT OPPORTUNITIES THAT ALIGN WITH MY PROFESSIONAL GOALS & VALUES

I AM VALUABLE TO MY ORGANIZATION AND MY CONTRIBUTIONS MAKE A POSITIVE IMPACT

I EMBRACE CHALLENGES IN MY CAREER AS OPPORTUNITIES TO GROW AND EXCEL

I AM A NATURAL LEADER INSPIRING OTHERS WITH MY WORK ETHIC & VISION

I CONTINUOUSLY IMPROVE MY KNOWLEDGE AND SKILLS TO STAY AHEAD IN MY FIELD

MY CAREER SUCCESS IS A REFLECTION OF MY DEDICATION & RESILIENCE HARD WORK

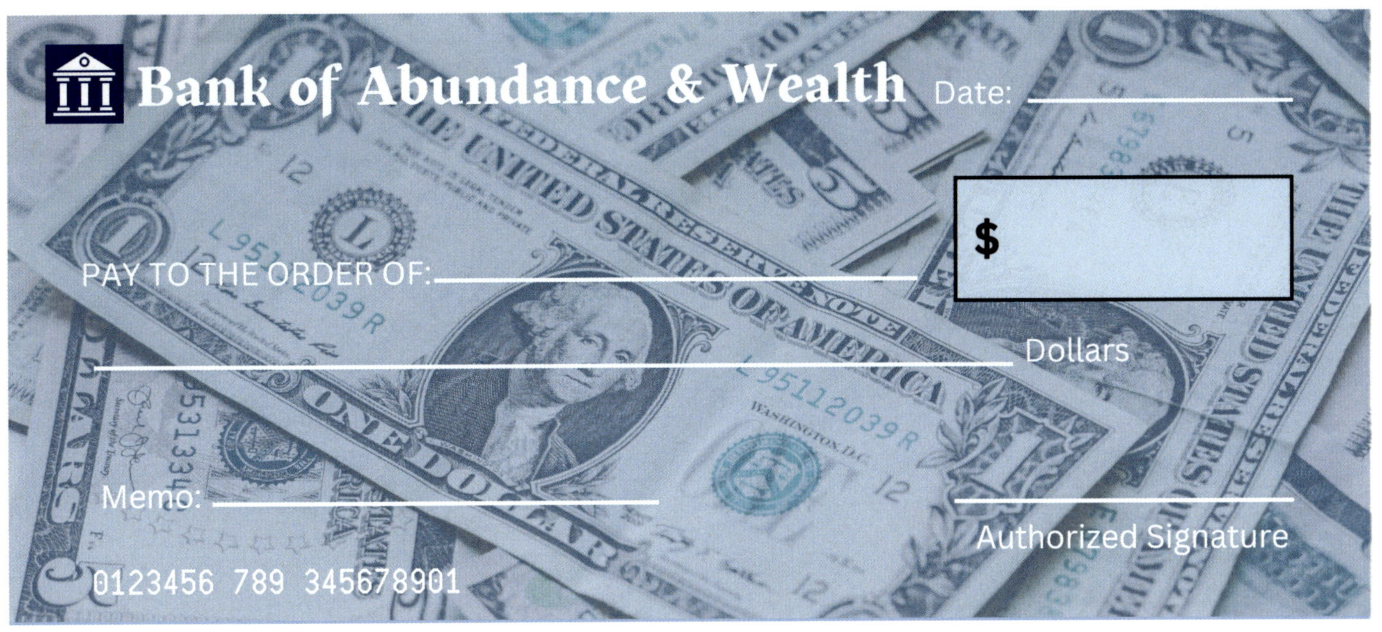
Bank of Abundance & Wealth
Date:
$
PAY TO THE ORDER OF:
Dollars
Memo:
Authorized Signature
0123456 789 345678901

Bank of Abundance & Wealth
Date:
£
PAY TO THE ORDER OF:
Pounds
Memo:
Authorised Signature
0123456 789 345678901

Bank of Abundance & Wealth
Date:
$
PAY TO THE ORDER OF:
Dollars
Memo:
Authorized Signature
0123456 789 345678901

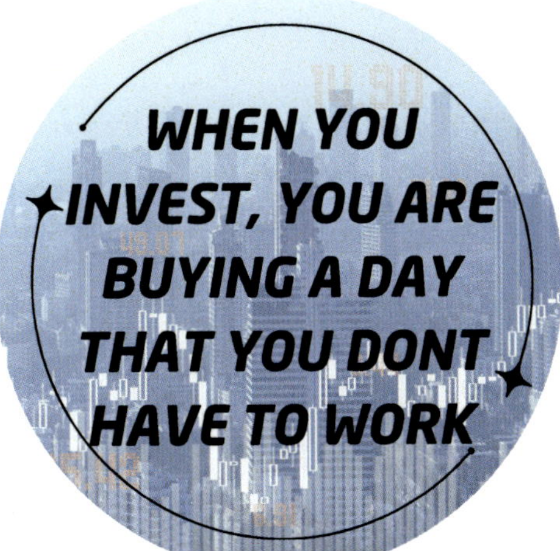

MONEYFESTING

INVESTMENT

I INVEST SUCCESSFULLY AND CONSISTENTLY

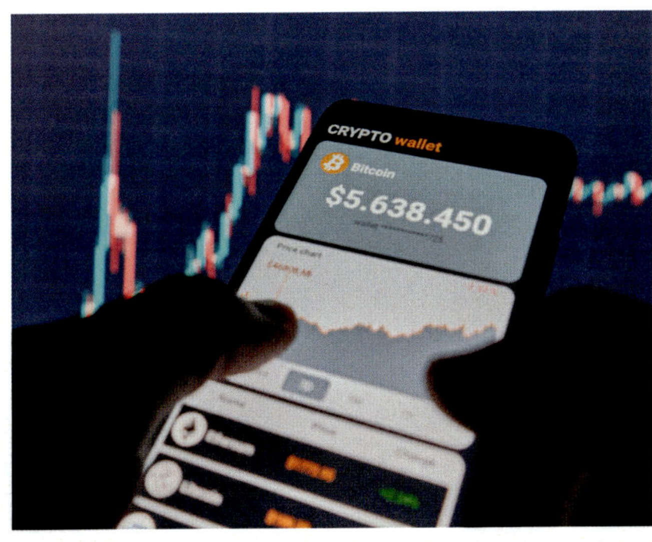

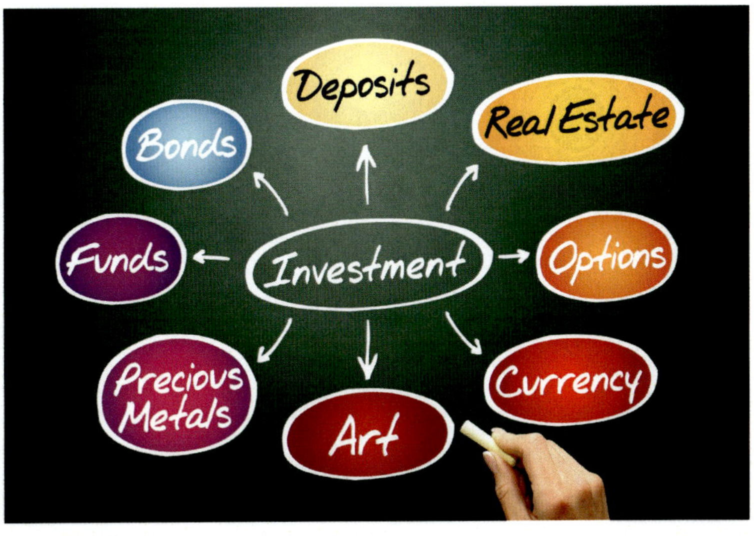

SAVINGS THIS YEAR:

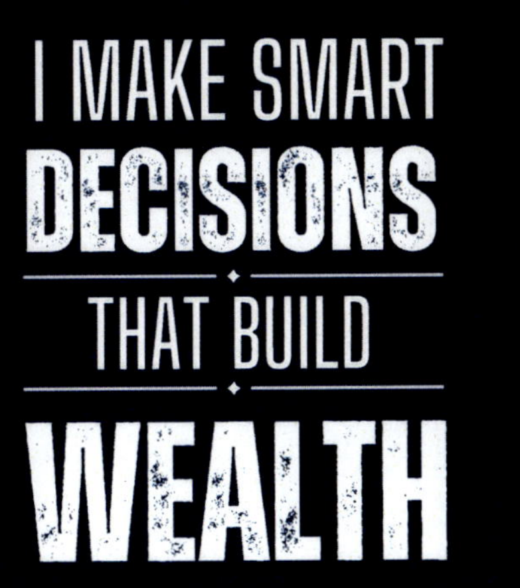

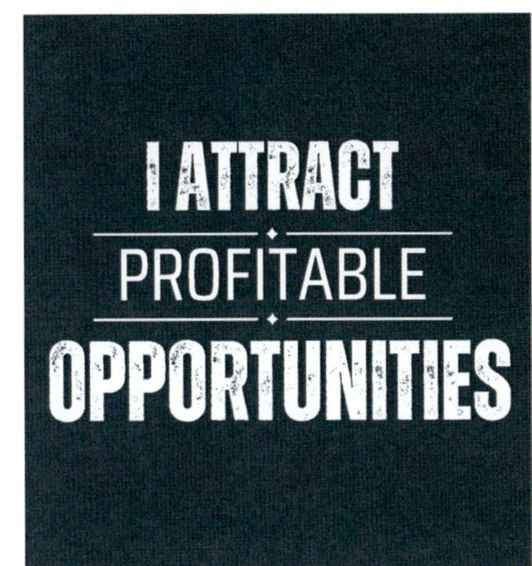

I AM
DISCIPLINED
IN MANAGING
MY FINANCES

I CREATE
MULTIPLE STREAMS
OF INCOME
TO ACHIEVE
FINANCIAL
FREEDOM

I AM FOCUSED
MOTIVATED AND
COMMITTED
TO GROWING MY
FINANCIAL
PORTFOLIO

I DESERVE
FINANCIAL
SUCCESS AND
I WORK
DILIGENTLY TO
ACHIEVE IT

I SAVE INVEST
AND SPEND
MY MONEY WISELY
BUILDING A SECURE
FUTURE FOR MYSELF
AND MY FAMILY

I CONSISTENTLY
INCREASE MY
INCOME BY
DELIVERING VALUE
AND SEIZING NEW
OPPORTUNITIES

I HANDLE
MY MONEY
WITH CONFIDENCE
AND CLARITY
CREATING LONG-TERM
WEALTH

I AM ON
THE PATH TO
FINANCIAL
INDEPENDENCE

MY FINANCIAL
MINDSET
IS ONE OF
ABUNDANCE
GROWTH AND
PROSPERITY

ARRIVED

ARRIVED

ARRIVED

ARRIVED

ARRIVED

ARRIVED

ARRIVED

WORLD
PASSPORT

ARRIVED

ARRIVED

ARRIVED

ARRIVED

ARRIVED

ARRIVED

ARRIVED

ARRIVED

ARRIVED

ARRIVED

ARRIVED

ARRIVED

ARRIVED

ARRIVED

ARRIVED

ARRIVED

ARRIVED

GERMANY

MALAYSIA

CANADA

ITALY

INDONESIA

NORWAY

IRELAND

SINGAPORE

BRAZIL

GREAT
BRITAIN

CHINA

COLUMBIA

FRANCE
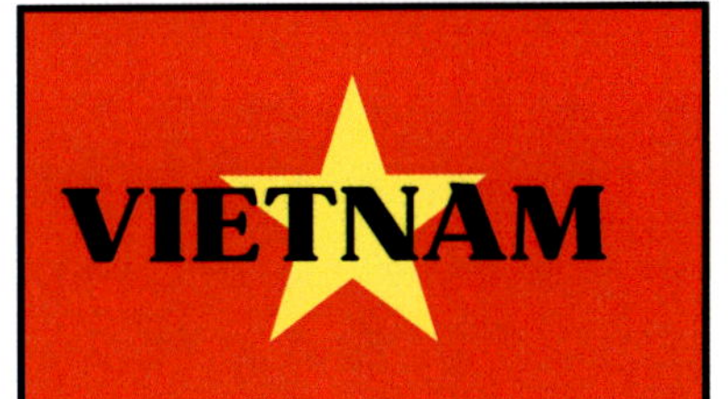
VIETNAM

ARGENTINA

SPAIN

THAILAND

ICELAND

GREECE

INDIA

AUSTRALI
A

AUSTRIA

JAPAN

MEXICO

EVERY JOURNEY I TAKE ENRICHES MY LIFE AND BROADENS MY PERSPECTIVE

I ATTRACT AMAZING TRAVEL OPPORTUNITIES THAT ALIGN WITH MY DREAMS

I AM COURAGEOUS IN STEPPING OUT OF MY COMFORT ZONE WHILE TRAVELING

MY TRAVEL EXPERIENCES CREATE LASTING MEMORIES & PERSONAL GROWTH

I AM WORTHY OF TAKING TIME FOR MYSELF TO EXPLORE THE WORLD

MY TRAVEL BUDGET GROWS AS I PRIORITIZE MY WANDERLUST

I EMBRACE SPONTANEITY AND ALLOW ADVENTURES TO UNFOLD NATURALLY

I CONNECT DEEPLY WITH PEOPLE I MEET ON MY TRAVELS

I ATTRACT POSITIVE ENERGY AND ADVENTURE WHEREVER I GO

I AM A CONFIDENT ADVENTUROUS TRAVELER READY FOR ANY CHALLENGE

MY TRAVEL DREAMS ARE WITHIN REACH AND WILL ACHIEVE THEM

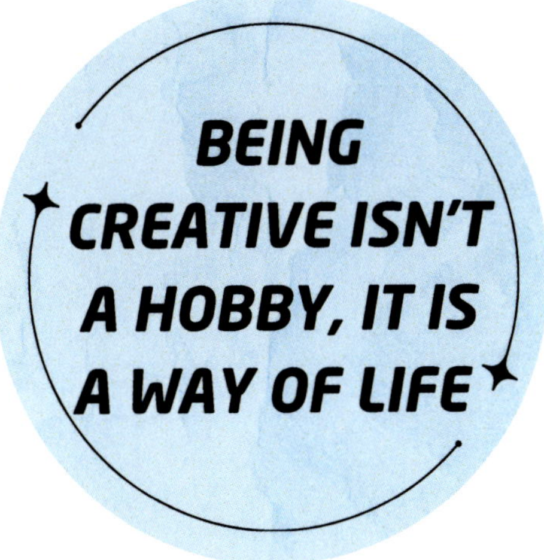
BEING
CREATIVE ISN'T
A HOBBY, IT IS
A WAY OF LIFE

PRACTICE DAILY

I EMBRACE MY PASSIONS AND DEDICATE TIME TO MY HOBBIES

I AM COMMITTED TO EXPLORING NEW HOBBIES THAT DRIVE ME

MY CREATIVITY FLOWS FREELY AS I ENGAGE IN ACTIVITIES I LOVE

EACH MOMENT SPENT ON MY HOBBIES BRINGS ME JOY FULFILLMENT & PURPOSE

I AM OPEN TO DISCOVERING NEW TALENTS AND INTERESTS WITHIN MYSELF

I FIND BALANCE IN MY LIFE BY PRIORITIZING MY PERSONAL INTERESTS

I MAKE TIME FOR MY PASSIONS KNOWING THEY ENRICH MY LIFE

I EARN AND GROW THROUGH MY HOBBIES EXPANDING MY KNOWLEDGE & SKILLS

I AM PROUD OF THE TIME AND EFFORT I INVEST IN MY HOBBIES

I ALLOW MYSELF TO BE PLAYFUL AND ADVENTUROUS IN MY PURSUITS

MY HOBBIES INSPIRE ME TO LIVE A MORE VIBRANT AND FULFILLING LIFE

I APPROACH EACH HOBBY WITH CURIOSITY & ENTHUSIASM

I WOULD RATHER DIE OF PASSION THAN OF BOREDOM